Starting from Zero

A Guide to Making Money from Scratch
Jules Beshears

Contents

1.

2.

3.

4.

5.

6.

7.

8.

9.

10.

11.

12.

13.

Message From The Author

"Iwas told we are paid for our value and not our time." As such, my books, on the surface, may seem somewhat lacking in terms of page count. What they lack in the sheer number of pages that tell stories about me growing up, or making my first million, etc., I choose to prioritize value. The books I write remove most of the fluff and are condensed, distilled, raw value that will hopefully change your life for the better.

This book is dedicated to my family, friends, and to all the entrepreneurs that chose never to give up.

Chapter 1

Introduction: Understanding the Mindset of Successful Entrepreneurs

Starting a business from scratch requires a unique set of skills, qualities, and a specific mindset. This chapter explores the key characteristics and traits that make successful entrepreneurs successful. Whether you're just starting or have been running a business for a while, understanding the mindset of successful entrepreneurs can help you stay motivated and focused on your goals.

Successful entrepreneurs have a few things in common:

- A willingness to take risks.
- An unwavering belief in their abilities and ideas.
- An insatiable appetite for learning.

They also understand that success is not a destination but a journey that requires hard work, perseverance, and an unrelenting pursuit of excellence.

They have a clear vision for their future, are not afraid to dream big, and set high goals. At the same time, they are also practical and strategic in their approach and understand the importance of planning and executing their ideas precisely.

Another key trait of successful entrepreneurs is their ability to handle uncertainty and unpredictability. The world of business is constantly changing, and successful entrepreneurs can adapt quickly to new challenges and opportunities. They understand that setbacks and failures are part of the journey, and they use these experiences to refine their strategies and build their resilience.

Successful entrepreneurs also have a strong network of professional and personal support. They understand the value of collaboration and are open to asking for help. They also invest in personal and professional development, seeking opportunities to improve their skills and knowledge.

Moreover, successful entrepreneurs have a growth mindset. They see challenges as opportunities for growth and are constantly seeking new ways to improve their businesses. They also understand the importance of being open to feedback and are willing to change their strategies as needed.

Finally, successful entrepreneurs have a deep sense of purpose and drive. They are motivated by their passions and have a strong desire to positively impact their communities and the world. This drive and determination help them overcome obstacles and continue pushing forward, even in the face of adversity.

The mindset of successful entrepreneurs is a combination of self-belief, resilience, flexibility, continuous learning, collaboration, growth, and purpose. By embracing these qualities and developing them, you can set yourself up for success and build a thriving business   from   scratch.

Chapter 2

Assessing Your Skills and Interests for Potential Business Opportunities

Before starting a business, you must understand what you bring to the table regarding skills and interests. This chapter will help you assess your strengths and determine the types of companies that best align with your skills and passions.

Step 1: Identify Your Skills

The first step in assessing your skills is creating a comprehensive list of everything you're good at and enjoy doing. This can include technical skills, such as graphic design or coding, as well as soft skills, such as communication or leadership. Be bold and include things that may seem trivial, as every skill can be valuable in business.

Step 2: Evaluate Your Interests

Next, evaluate your interests and think about the types of activities or hobbies that you enjoy. This can give you a clue as to the types of businesses that will be a good fit for you. For example, if you're an avid gardener, starting a landscaping business or a garden center may be a good fit for you.

Step 3: Conduct Market Research

Once you have a list of your skills and interests, it's time to conduct market research. Look for businesses that align with your skills and interests and assess the potential demand for those businesses. Consider factors such as market saturation, competition, and profitability.

Step 4: Consider Your Passions

In addition to your skills and interests, it's essential to consider your passions. What drives you, and what do you care about deeply? Starting a business that aligns with your passions will not only increase your chances of success, but it will also bring you joy and fulfillment.

Step 5: Determine Your Unique Selling Proposition (USP)

Finally, consider what sets you apart from others in your field. What are your unique skills and experiences that can be leveraged in your business? Your USP will be crucial in differentiating yourself from competitors and making your business stand out.

Step 6: Seek Out Mentors and Advisors

Once you clearly understand your skills, interests, and passions, it can be helpful to seek out mentors and advisors with experience in the type of business you're interested in starting. They can provide valuable insight and guidance and help you avoid common pitfalls. Consider reaching out to successful entrepreneurs in your field, joining professional organizations, or participating in business incubators or accelerators.

Step 7: Test Your Ideas

Before committing to a business, testing your ideas and getting feedback from potential customers can be helpful. This can be done through market research, focus groups, or launching a small-scale pilot project. This can help validate your ideas and better understand your product or service demand.

Step 8: Consider Your Resources

When assessing your skills and interests, it's important to consider the resources you have available to you. This can include financial resources, personal connections, and access to technology and equipment. Understanding your available resources will help you determine which business opportunities are feasible and which may require additional investment.

Step 9: Be Flexible and Adaptable

It's important to remember that the business landscape is constantly changing, and your interests and skills may also change. Be open to exploring new opportunities as they arise, and be willing to pivot your strategy if needed. Successful entrepreneurs are flexible and adaptable and understand that the journey to success may not always be a straight line.

In conclusion, assessing your skills and interests is an ongoing process that requires self-reflection and a willingness to learn and grow. By taking the time to understand your strengths, passions, and market demand, you can increase your chances of success and build a business that you love. Remember to be flexible and adaptable, seek mentorship and guidance, and continuously evaluate and test your ideas to ensure you're on the right track.

Chapter 3

Building a Strong Foundation: Budgeting, Saving, and Investing

Starting a business requires significant time, energy, and resources. To be successful, it's crucial to have a solid financial foundation in place. This chapter will explore the importance of budgeting, saving, and investing and provide practical tips for building a strong financial foundation for your business.

Budgeting

Budgeting is the process of creating a plan for how you will allocate your income and expenses. It's a crucial step in managing your finances and ensuring the long-term success of your business. When creating a budget, it's important to consider your fixed expenses, such as rent and utilities, as well as your variable expenses, such as supplies and marketing. Additionally, you should set aside funds for unexpected expenses and the growth and expansion of your business.

To create a budget, follow these steps:

1. Identify all of your income sources
2. List all of your fixed expenses
3. List all of your variable expenses
4. Determine your monthly and annual expenses
5. Set financial goals and allocate funds towards those goals
6. Continuously monitor and adjust your budget as needed

Saving

Saving is a critical component of building a solid financial foundation. It allows you to prepare for unexpected expenses and helps ensure the long-term stability of your business. When starting a business, it's vital to have an emergency fund with at least six months of living expenses saved. This will help you weather any unexpected financial challenges that may arise.

In addition to an emergency fund, it's important to regularly set aside a portion of your income for savings. This can help you reach your financial goals, such as buying equipment, expanding your business, or investing in your future.

Investing

Investing is another important component of building a solid financial foundation. It allows you to grow your wealth over time and prepare for retirement. When starting a business, it's essential to consider the various available investments, such as stocks, bonds, and real estate.

It's important to consult with a financial advisor and conduct research before making any investment decisions. Additionally, it's essential to consider your personal financial goals and risk tolerance when making investment decisions.

In conclusion, budgeting, saving, and investing are essential components of building a strong financial foundation for your business. By taking the time to create a budget, regularly save, and make informed investment decisions, you can ensure your business's long-term success and stability.

Chapter 4

Finding and Validating a Business Idea

Finding a viable business idea is the first step toward starting a successful venture. Finding an idea that aligns with your skills, interests, passions, and market demand are important. In this chapter, we will explore the process of finding and validating a business idea and provide you with tips and tools to help you get started.

Step 1: Identify Your Passion and Skills

The first step in finding a business idea is identifying your passions and skills. This can be done through self-reflection and market research. Consider what you enjoy doing and what you're good at, and think about how those skills and interests can be applied to a business.

Step 2: Research Market Demand

Once you have a general idea of the type of business you'd like to start, it's crucial to research market demand. This can be done by conducting market research, reaching out to potential customers, and analyzing industry trends.

Step 3: Validate Your Idea

Before committing to a business idea, it's important to validate it through market research and customer feedback. This can be done by conducting surveys, focus groups, or launching a small-scale pilot project. This helps you understand the demand for your products or services and validate the viability of your business idea.

Step 4: Refine Your Business Concept

Based on the feedback you receive from your market research, you may need to refine your business concept. This can involve tweaking your product or service offering, adjusting your target market, or changing your marketing and sales strategy.

Step 5: Develop a Business Plan

Once you clearly understand your business idea and the demand for your products or services, it's time to develop a business plan. A business plan is a comprehensive document that outlines your business concept, target market, marketing and sales strategy, and financial projections.

Networking and seeking feedback from experienced entrepreneurs, business advisors, and mentors is another crucial step in finding and validating a business idea. These individuals can provide valuable insights and advice and help you identify potential challenges and opportunities.

Step 7: Consider Your Competition

It's also important to consider your competition when finding and validating a business idea. Researching your competitors can help you understand the market and identify areas where you can differentiate your business. This can help you stand out in a crowded market and increase your chances of success.

Step 8: Test Your Idea

Before launching your business, it's important to test your idea. This can involve launching a small-scale pilot project, offering a limited version of your product or service, or seeking pre-orders from customers. This allows you to validate your business idea and identify potential challenges before fully committing to your venture.

In conclusion, finding and validating a business idea is a critical step in the process of starting a successful venture. By following these steps, you can increase your chances of success and build a business that you love. Additionally, seeking feedback, considering your competition, and testing your idea can help you identify potential challenges and opportunities and ensure that your business is on the right track.

Chapter 5

Networking and Marketing on a Tight Budget

Marketing and networking are critical components of a successful business, but they can also be expensive. As a startup or small business, you may have a small marketing budget, but you can still effectively promote your business and reach your target market. In this chapter, we will explore strategies for networking and marketing on a tight budget.

Step 1: Utilize Free Marketing Channels

There are several free marketing channels that you can utilize to promote your business, including social media, content marketing, and search engine optimization (SEO). These channels allow you to reach a large audience without spending much money, and they can be highly effective when used correctly.

Step 2: Leverage Word of Mouth

Word of mouth is one of the most potent forms of marketing, and it doesn't cost a thing. Encourage your existing customers to spread the word about your business and give them incentives, such as discounts or referral bonuses.

Step 3: Attend Networking Events

Attending networking events is a great way to connect with potential customers and partners and can also be an effective marketing tool. Look for networking events in your industry, and be prepared to make a strong impression.

Step 4: Collaborate with Other Businesses

Collaborating with other businesses is a great way to reach a new audience and promote your business. Consider partnering with complementary businesses to cross-promote each other's products or services.

Step 5: Offer Promotions and Discounts

Offering promotions and discounts is another effective way to promote your business and attract new customers. This can be done through email marketing, social media, or even in-person events.

Step 6: Create a Strong Online Presence

Having a robust online presence is essential in today's digital age. Ensure your website is professional, easy to navigate, and optimized for search engines. Also, consider creating profiles on relevant social media platforms, and make sure that your business information is up-to-date and consistent across all platforms.

Step 7: Use Influencer Marketing

Influencer marketing involves partnering with individuals who have a large following on social media and paying them to promote your business. This can be an effective way to reach a new audience, and it's often more affordable than traditional advertising.

Step 8: Participate in Local Community Events

Participating in local community events is another excellent way to promote your business and connect with potential customers. Look for events in your area that align with your target market, and consider exhibiting or sponsoring the event.

Step 9: Utilize Email Marketing

Email marketing is a cost-effective way to reach a large audience and promote your business. Build an email list of customers and potential customers, and use it to send regular updates, promotions, and special offers.

Step 10: Focus on Quality Over Quantity

Regarding marketing and networking, it's essential to focus on quality over quantity. Instead of reaching a large audience, focus on reaching the right audience. This will help you build more meaningful connections and achieve better results.

In conclusion, marketing and networking are critical components of a successful business and don't have to be expensive. By utilizing free marketing channels, leveraging word of mouth, attending networking events, collaborating with other companies, offering promotions and discounts, creating a strong online presence, using influencer marketing, participating in local community events, utilizing email marketing, and focusing on quality over quantity, you can effectively promote your business and reach your target market, even on a tight budget.

Chapter 6

Launching Your Business: The Do's and Don'ts

Launching a business can be an exciting and challenging process. To ensure the success of your business, it's essential to understand the do's and don'ts of launching a new business. In this chapter, we will explore some of the key considerations when establishing your business.

Do's:

1. Plan Thoroughly: Before launching your business, take the time to develop a comprehensive business plan. This should include an overview of your business, your target market, your competition, and your marketing and sales strategies.

2. Build a Strong Team: Surround yourself with talented and dedicated individuals who share your passion for your business. This may include employees, partners, or consultants.

3. Utilize Social Media: Utilize social media to promote your business and connect with your target market. Choose platforms that align with your target market, and create a consistent and professional online presence.

4. Focus on Customer Service: Customer service is vital to the success of your business. Make sure that your employees are trained to provide excellent customer service and that your customers feel valued and appreciated.

5. Network and Collaborate: Networking and collaborating with other businesses and individuals is an important component of launching a successful business. Attend events, participate in online communities, and look for opportunities to collaborate with complementary businesses.

Don'ts:

1. Ignore Your Competition: Don't ignore your competition. Take the time to understand their strengths and weaknesses, and develop strategies to differentiate your business and capture market share.

2. Overlook Legal Considerations: Don't overlook legal considerations when launching your business. This may include obtaining the proper licenses, permits, and insurance, as well as protecting your intellectual property.

3. Underestimate the Importance of Cash Flow: Don't underestimate the importance of cash flow. Make sure you have enough capital to cover your expenses and maintain a healthy cash flow, especially during the early stages of your business.

4. Launch Without a Marketing Plan: Don't launch your business without a marketing plan. Make sure that you have a clear understanding of your target market and a plan for how you will reach and engage with them.

5. Neglect to Stay Organized: Don't neglect to stay organized. Keep detailed records of your finances, sales, and expenses, and use tools and software to help you stay organized and on top of your business.

Chapter 7

Scaling Your Business: Strategies for Growth

Once your business is up and running, it's important to think about scaling and growing your business. In this chapter, we will explore some strategies you can use to scale your business and achieve growth.

1. Diversify Your Products or Services: Diversifying your products or services can help you reach new customers and increase your revenue. Consider adding complementary products or services that complement your existing offerings.

2. Expand Your Reach: Expanding your reach can help you reach new customers and increase your sales. Consider expanding into new markets, either domestically or internationally.

3. Enhance Your Marketing and Sales Efforts: Enhancing your marketing and sales efforts can help you reach new customers and increase sales. Consider investing in digital marketing, such as search engine optimization (SEO), pay-per-click advertising (PPC), and social media marketing.

4. Optimize Your Operations: Optimizing your operations can help you increase efficiency, reduce costs, and improve the customer experience. Consider investing in technology, such as customer relationship management (CRM) software, and streamlining your processes.

5. Foster a Culture of Innovation: Foster a culture of innovation by encouraging employees to be creative and think outside the box. This can help you stay ahead of the curve and find new and innovative ways to grow your business.

6. Seek Out Partnerships and Joint Ventures: Seek out partnerships and joint ventures with complementary businesses. This can help you leverage each other's strengths and reach new customers.

7. Stay Ahead of Trends: Stay ahead of trends by continually researching and staying informed about industry developments. This can help you identify new opportunities for growth and stay ahead of your competition.

In conclusion, scaling your business is an important step in achieving growth and success. By implementing these strategies, you can increase your chances of success and achieve your business goals.

Chapter 8

Managing Cash Flow and Financing Your Business

Managing cash flow and financing your business are crucial aspects of running a successful business. In this chapter, we will explore strategies you can use to manage your cash flow and finance your business.

1. Manage Your Cash Flow: To manage your cash flow, you need to understand when money is coming in and going out. You should also be prepared for unexpected expenses and have a contingency plan.

2. Utilize Invoicing and Payment Systems: Utilizing invoicing and payment systems can help you receive payments faster and more efficiently. Consider using an invoicing and payment system that integrates with your accounting software.

3. Seek Out Alternative Financing Options: Seek out alternative financing options such as small business loans, grants, or equity financing. This can help you raise the capital you need to grow your business.

4. Manage Your Debt: Managing your debt is important for maintaining a healthy cash flow. Consider paying off high-interest debt first and prioritize paying off debt overtaking new debt.

5. Build an Emergency Fund: Building an emergency fund can help you manage unexpected expenses and maintain a stable

cash flow. Consider setting aside a portion of your monthly revenue to build an emergency fund.

6. Seek Out Professional Advice: Seeking out professional advice from a financial advisor or accountant can help you make informed decisions about managing your cash flow and financing your business.

7. Utilize Cost-Saving Strategies: Utilizing cost-saving strategies can help you conserve cash and improve your bottom line. Consider reducing expenses by negotiating with suppliers, automating processes, and outsourcing non-essential tasks.

8. Monitor Your Finances: Monitoring your finances regularly is crucial for managing your cash flow and ensuring that your business is financially stable. Consider setting up a system for tracking your finances and reviewing your financial statements regularly.

9. Consider Invoicing and Receiving Payments in Advance: Consider invoicing and receiving payments in advance to help ensure a steady flow of cash into your business. This can be particularly useful for businesses with long payment cycles.

10. Take Advantage of Tax Credits and Deductions: Take advantage of tax credits and deductions to reduce your tax bill and conserve cash. Consider seeking the advice of a tax professional to determine which credits and deductions are available to your business.

11. Stay On Top of Invoices and Payment Due Dates: Stay on top of invoices and payment due dates to ensure that you receive payments in a timely manner. Consider setting reminders and

automating the invoicing process to help streamline the process.

12. Plan for Seasonal Fluctuations in Cash Flow: Plan for seasonal fluctuations in cash flow by anticipating when your business is likely to experience an influx or a slowdown in revenue. This can help you plan ahead and manage your cash flow more effectively.

Managing cash flow and financing your business are important aspects of running a successful business. By implementing these strategies, you can improve your cash flow, secure the funding you need to grow your business, and ensure that your business is financially   stable.

Chapter 9

Optimizing Your Business for Growth and Profitability

Optimizing your business for growth and profitability is crucial for ensuring its long-term success. In this chapter, we will explore some of the strategies you can use to optimize your business for growth and profitability.

1. Focus on Your Core Competencies: Focusing on your core competencies can help you differentiate your business from the competition and improve your profitability. Consider identifying your strengths and areas for improvement and then focusing on your strengths to build a competitive advantage.

2. Embrace Innovation and Technology: Embracing innovation and technology can help you stay ahead of the competition and improve efficiency. Consider investing in technology that will help you automate processes, improve customer experience, and streamline operations.

3. Diversify Your Product and Service Offerings: Diversifying your product and service offerings can help you reach new markets and reduce your reliance on a single product or service. Consider researching new markets and identifying new products or services that you can offer to your customers.

4. Build Strong Relationships with Your Customers: Building strong relationships with your customers is key to retaining their business and attracting new customers. Consider providing excellent customer service, building a loyal

customer base, and seeking feedback from your customers to continuously improve your offerings.

5. Invest in Employee Training and Development: Investing in employee training and development can help you improve employee productivity and satisfaction. Consider offering training programs, mentorship opportunities, and professional development opportunities to help your employees grow and develop.

6. Streamline Your Operations: Streamlining your operations can help you reduce expenses and improve efficiency. Consider identifying areas for improvement and implementing process improvements, such as automating tasks, outsourcing non-essential tasks, and reducing waste.

7. Monitor Your Key Performance Indicators (KPIs): Monitoring your key performance indicators (KPIs) can help you understand the health of your business and identify areas for improvement. Consider tracking metrics such as revenue, customer satisfaction, and employee satisfaction to measure your performance and identify areas for improvement.

8. Stay on Top of Market Trends: Staying on top of market trends can help you stay ahead of the competition and identify new opportunities. Consider conducting market research, attending trade shows, and staying up-to-date with industry news to stay informed.

9. Continuously Evaluate and Adapt Your Strategy: Continuously evaluating and adapting your strategy is essential for staying ahead of the competition and responding to changes in the market. Consider regularly reviewing your

business plan and making adjustments as necessary. Additionally, consider conducting market research and seeking feedback from customers to stay informed of changes in customer needs and preferences.

10. Manage Your Finances Effectively: Effective financial management is crucial for maximizing profitability and minimizing risk. Consider implementing effective budgeting and accounting practices, regularly monitoring your cash flow, and seeking professional advice when necessary. Additionally, consider seeking funding opportunities, such as loans or investments, to help grow your business.

11. Leverage Online Marketing: Leveraging online marketing can help you reach a wider audience and promote your business effectively. Consider implementing a digital marketing strategy that includes a website, social media presence, and search engine optimization (SEO) tactics. Additionally, consider using online advertising to reach your target audience and promote your products or services.

12. Collaborate with Other Businesses: Collaborating with other businesses can help you expand your reach and benefit from each other's expertise. Consider identifying complementary businesses and forming partnerships to cross-promote products and services and pool resources. Additionally, consider joining local business networks and organizations to connect with other entrepreneurs and business owners.

13. Foster a Positive Work Culture: Foster a positive work culture to improve employee morale and retain top talent. Consider creating a supportive and inclusive work environment,

recognizing and rewarding employee contributions, and promoting work-life balance. Additionally, consider investing in employee wellness programs and benefits to improve employee satisfaction and well-being.

14. Plan for Succession: Planning for succession is crucial for ensuring the long-term success of your business. Consider developing a succession plan that outlines the steps for transferring ownership and management responsibilities to a successor. Additionally, consider grooming future leaders and developing a strong leadership team to help support the transition.

Optimizing your business for growth and profitability requires a combination of strategy, focus, and hard work. By following these best practices, you can create a strong foundation for success and set your business on a path to long-term growth and profitability.

Chapter 10

Managing Your Business Finances: Budgeting, Taxation, and Record-keeping

Effective financial management is a critical component of running a successful business. From budgeting and tax planning to record-keeping and cash flow management, it's essential to have a comprehensive understanding of your finances to maximize profitability and minimize risk. This chapter will explore key financial management practices for small business owners.

Budgeting and Forecasting

Budgeting and forecasting are essential tools for managing your finances and staying on top of your expenses. A budget helps you plan and control your spending, while a forecast helps you anticipate future expenses and revenue. When creating your budget, consider the following tips:

1. Start with your fixed expenses: Fixed expenses are costs that remain the same each month, such as rent and utilities. These expenses should be the first items included in your budget.

2. Track your variable expenses: Variable expenses are costs that change each month, such as supplies and marketing expenses. Keeping track of these expenses will help you identify areas where you can make cuts to improve your bottom line.

3. Factor in unexpected expenses: Unexpected expenses are costs that can arise unexpectedly, such as equipment repairs or legal fees. To prepare for these expenses, consider setting

aside a portion of your revenue each month into a contingency fund.

4. Update your budget regularly: Your budget should be a living document that you regularly update as your business changes. Consider revisiting your budget monthly or quarterly to make sure it remains accurate and relevant.

Tax Planning

Tax planning is important in managing your finances and minimizing your tax liability. When it comes to taxes, consider the following tips:

1. Stay informed about tax laws: Stay up-to-date on the latest tax laws and regulations to ensure that you are in compliance and minimize your tax liability.

2. Plan ahead for tax time: Plan ahead for tax time by keeping accurate records and seeking professional advice when necessary.

3. Take advantage of tax deductions: Take advantage of tax deductions, such as those for business expenses, to minimize your taxable income and reduce your tax liability.

4. Consider hiring a tax professional: Consider hiring a tax professional to help you navigate the complex tax laws and regulations, especially if you are unfamiliar with the tax system.

Record-keeping

Accurate record-keeping is essential for managing your finances and staying on top of your expenses. Consider the following tips for effective record-keeping:

1. Keep accurate records: Keep accurate records of all of your business transactions, including expenses, revenue, and investments.

2. Use accounting software: Consider using accounting software to help manage your finances and keep accurate records. This software can automate many of the manual tasks involved in record-keeping and can provide you with real-time financial data.

3. Stay organized: Stay organized by keeping all of your financial records in one place and regularly updating them.

4. Seek professional advice: Seek professional advice, such as from an accountant, if you are unsure about the best way to manage your finances or keep accurate records.

Cash Flow Management

Cash flow management is the process of tracking and managing the movement of money in and out of your business. Effective cash flow management is crucial to ensure you have sufficient funds to pay expenses and invest in growth opportunities. Consider the following tips for effective cash flow management:

1. Monitor your cash flow regularly: Regularly monitor your cash flow to ensure that you have enough funds available to cover your expenses and take advantage of growth opportunities.

2. Prioritize payment of bills: Prioritize payment of bills to avoid late fees and maintain good credit.

3. Manage accounts payable and receivable: Manage your accounts payable and receivable to ensure that you have

enough funds available to pay bills and receive payments from customers on time.

4. Consider using invoicing and payment tools: Consider using invoicing and payment tools, such as online payment systems, to streamline your cash flow management and improve your ability to receive payments on time.

5. Keep an emergency fund: Keep an emergency fund to provide a safety net in case of unexpected expenses or revenue shortfalls.

Investing in Your Business

Investing in your business is crucial for growth and profitability. Consider the following tips for effective investment:

1. Set aside a portion of revenue for investment: Set aside a portion of your revenue each month for investment in your business.

2. Evaluate investment opportunities: Evaluate investment opportunities, such as hiring additional employees or expanding your product line, to determine their potential impact on your business.

3. Consider seeking outside funding: Consider seeking outside funding, such as a loan or investment from a venture capital firm, to provide additional resources for investment in your business.

4. Monitor the results of your investments: Monitor the results of your investments to ensure that they are generating a positive return and contributing to the growth and profitability of your business.

Effective financial management, including budgeting, tax planning, record-keeping, cash flow management, and investing, is crucial for running a successful business. By following these tips, you can ensure that your finances are under control and that you are in a strong position to take advantage of growth opportunities and maximize profitability.

Chapter 11

Staying Ahead of the Game: Continuous Learning and Adaptation

As an entrepreneur, it's essential to continuously learn and adapt to stay ahead of the competition and be relevant in the ever-changing business world. The following are tips for continuous learning and adaptation:

1. Stay informed about industry trends: Stay informed about industry trends and developments to understand the industry's direction and identify growth opportunities.

2. Attend industry events and conferences: Attend industry events and conferences to network with peers, learn about new trends and technologies, and stay up-to-date with the latest developments in your industry.

3. Read and educate yourself: Read books, articles, and other educational materials related to your industry to continuously expand your knowledge and gain new insights.

4. Seek feedback from customers: Seek feedback from customers to understand their needs and preferences and to identify areas where your business can improve.

5. Experiment with new ideas: Experiment with new ideas and strategies to continuously evolve and improve your business.

6. Hire a diverse team: Hire a diverse team with different backgrounds and skills to bring new perspectives and ideas to the table.

7. Collaborate with other businesses: Collaborate with other businesses in your industry to share knowledge and insights and to identify opportunities for growth and innovation.

8. Continuously reassess and adjust your strategy: Continuously reassess and adjust your strategy to ensure that you are on track to achieve your goals and stay ahead of the competition.

9. Mentorship and coaching: Seek out a mentor or coach to provide guidance, support, and advice on how to grow your business and develop your skills.

10. Surround yourself with successful individuals: Surround yourself with successful individuals who can offer insights and advice and who can help you grow both personally and professionally.

11. Take courses and workshops: Take courses and attend workshops to expand your knowledge and skills in areas relevant to your business.

12. Attend webinars and online events: Attend webinars and online events to learn from experts in your industry without leaving your office.

13. Join business organizations and networks: Join business organizations and networks to connect with other entrepreneurs and business owners and gain access to resources and support.

14. Embrace failure: Embrace failure as an opportunity to learn and grow. Use failures as lessons to identify areas where you can improve and become a better entrepreneur.

15. Stay open-minded: Stay open-minded and be willing to try new things. Don't be afraid to take risks and experiment with new ideas to find what works best for your business.

Continuous learning and adaptation are important not only for the success of your business but also for your personal growth and career advancement. By implementing these tips, you can ensure that you are always learning and evolving and that you are always staying ahead of the game.

Chapter 12

Conclusion: Sustaining Your Success and Inspiring Others

Starting a business from scratch is a challenging but rewarding journey, and it requires determination, hard work, and a growth mindset. By following the steps outlined in this book, you have taken the first steps toward building a successful business and achieving financial freedom.

In this chapter, we will discuss the importance of sustaining your success and inspiring others.

1. Celebrate your accomplishments: Take the time to celebrate your successes and acknowledge the hard work and dedication that went into building your business. Celebrating your accomplishments will give you a sense of pride and motivate you to continue on your journey.

2. Plan for the future: Plan for the future by setting new goals and developing a strategy for sustained growth and success. Continuously reassess your goals and make adjustments as needed to ensure that you are on track to achieve your long-term vision.

3. Stay disciplined and focused: Stay disciplined and focused on your goals, and continue to put in the hard work and effort required to sustain your success. Remember that success is a marathon, not a sprint, and it requires continuous effort and dedication.

4. Give back to your community: Give back to your community by volunteering, supporting local organizations, and mentoring aspiring entrepreneurs. By giving back, you can inspire others and make a positive impact in the world.

5. Share your story: Share your story and experiences with others to inspire and motivate them. By sharing your journey, you can provide hope and encouragement to those who are just starting out and help them to avoid common pitfalls and obstacles.

6. Continuously learn and grow: Continuously learn and grow by seeking out new challenges, taking courses and workshops, and reading books and articles. By continuously learning and growing, you can stay ahead of the game and continue to achieve success.

7. Surround yourself with supportive people: Surround yourself with supportive people who will encourage and motivate you and who will help you to stay focused and driven. Building a network of supportive friends, family members, mentors, and peers will help you to achieve your goals and overcome challenges.

8. Embrace change: Embrace change and be willing to adapt and pivot as needed. The business world is constantly changing, and it is important to be flexible and open to new ideas and opportunities. By embracing change, you can stay ahead of the curve and continue to achieve success.

9. Take care of yourself: Don't forget to take care of yourself both physically and mentally. It's important to prioritize self-

care and to engage in activities that help you to recharge and recharge your batteries. This will help you to stay focused and motivated and to continue to perform at your best.

10. Stay humble and grateful: Stay humble and grateful for your success, and never take it for granted. Remember that success is a journey, not a destination and that there will always be challenges and obstacles to overcome. By staying humble and grateful, you can continue to grow and develop, and you can inspire others to do the same.

In conclusion, sustaining your success and inspiring others requires a combination of hard work, dedication, and the right mindset. By following these tips and continuing to grow and develop, you can ensure that your business continues to thrive and that you are making a positive impact in the world. Whether you are just starting out or you are a seasoned entrepreneur, it is never too late to start making a difference and achieving your goals.

414 Industries Online Courses

https://414industries.com/

https://www.instagram.com/414industries/

https://www.facebook.com/414industries

www.ingramcontent.com/pod-product-compliance
Lightning Source LLC
Chambersburg PA
CBHW070758220526
45467CB00014B/760